# The Ultimate
# DICTIONARY
## of All Things
# DIGITAL

Illustrated by **ANNIKA BRANDOW**

dp
duopress

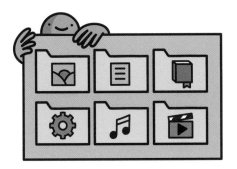

# DIGITAL

**DIH jeh tul • adjective**

having to do with, relating to, or using electronic technologies, tools, or devices that can store, send, or receive information through numbers

# A NOTE TO KIDS

Dear reader,

You've probably been using a computer since before you can remember. In fact, there might be one next to you right now. Whether it's a laptop, personal computer, phone, TV, car, refrigerator, traffic light, or another kind of technology, computers and digital devices are everywhere. We are interacting with them all the time!

But computer science and digital media are also always changing. New applications are being made, new programming languages are being invented, and more types of growth are happening in our lifetime that we might not even be able to imagine or comprehend. With these changes come changes to our daily lives and the need to adapt quickly to and process a wealth of information. It can get a little overwhelming! But knowledge is power. Once you have a grasp of the basics of our modern digital world, it can be much easier to learn more, have fun, and be safe while doing it.

In this book you'll learn all kinds of terms, but remember: Language changes, particularly in growing fields like technology. New things are being made and new words are being created all the time. If you have a question that's not covered in this book, do your research! Look it up or ask an adult to help you.

**And always remember the three big rules of digital responsibility:**

STAY SAFE...
BE SMART...
AND HAVE FUN!

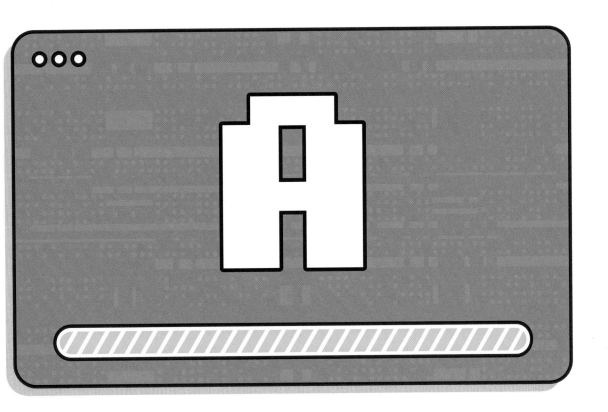

## ABSTRACTION
### ab STRAK shun • noun

the process of ignoring information that you don't need, in order to focus on the information you do need, to solve a problem

## AD BLOCKER
### AD - BLAH kur • noun

a browser plug-in (see page 34) that stops advertisements from showing up on a website

*It can be annoying and distracting to see so many advertisements on the internet! Ads can also slow down a website you're visiting or a video you want to watch. However, some websites make money from advertisements and may not receive funds when ads are blocked, so they may encourage you not to use an ad blocker.*

## ALGORITHM
### AL guh rih thum • noun

a step-by-step process followed when performing a task; for example, instructions that a computer program might follow (see Algorithms in Real Life, page 2)

## ALGORITHM BIAS
### AL guh rih thum — BYE us • noun

the errors in a computer system algorithm that systematically create unfair or unequal outcomes, such as giving one arbitrary group of users an advantage over others; can be due to incomplete, incorrect, or irrelevant data (see Budgeting for Bias, page 2)

*A school admissions algorithm, or a program set up to determine who should be admitted, may deny opportunities to certain students based on how the program was set up.*

## ANALOG

### ANN uh lahg • noun

not relating to computers; also describes a clock with hour and minute hands

*The opposite of analog is digital.*

## ANTIVIRUS SOFTWARE

### ant eye VIH russ — SOHFT ware • noun

a computer program that protects your computer or network against viruses or malware (see page 28)

## API

### A pee eye • noun

stands for: **application programming interface**

a dashboard, or a connection between two computers or two systems, that helps a user interact with an operating system or application

## APPLICATION

### app lih KAY shun • noun

software that is created to do something specific

*For example, word processors like Microsoft Word and Apple Pages are designed to help you write and format papers for homework. The term "app," the shortened version of "application," can also refer to programs on your phone, like an app that tells you the weather forecast.*

## ARRAY

### uh RAY • noun

a series or a group of the same type of elements that are organized in a specific order; values that are both integers and strings and are stored in an ordered list

## ARTIFICIAL INTELLIGENCE

**ahr tih FISH ul – ihn TELL ih gentz • noun**

the ability that a computer has to think, problem-solve, and learn (see Who Is Intelligent?, right); can be shortened to AI

## ASCII

**AS kee • noun**

stands for: **American Standard Code for Information Interchange**

a set of rules and standards on how text can be converted to and stored in binary code; also known as US-ASCII

*Fun fact: ASCII was developed from telegraph code.*

## ASSEMBLER

**ah SEHM blur • noun**

something that takes a low-level assembly language and translates it into machine code (see From Letters to Numbers, page 47)

## ATTACHMENT

**uh TACH ment • noun**

a file sent with an email message that can be downloaded and saved to your drive

## AUGMENTED REALITY

**AWG mehn tehd – ree AA lih tee • noun**

a view of a physical, real-world environment that has been enhanced with virtual elements using computer software; the popular game Pokémon Go is a good example of augmented reality

## AUGMENTED VIRTUALITY

**AWG mehn tehd – vihr choo AA lih tee • noun**

a view of a mostly computer-generated environment that can be manipulated by the user; for example, you can design your own room by selecting and moving virtual furniture, lamps, etc., around a digital version of your room

### DIG ⚙ DEEPER
### Who Is Intelligent?

When you think of AI (artificial intelligence), you might imagine a cinematic takeover of the world by human-like robots. But AI is a tool that can make our world easier or more fun. It can drive a car for you, compete against you in games like chess, or write poems or movie scripts. Someday it might be able to help doctors decide which treatment is best for cancer or become your personal assistant.

However, there will always be situations where humans will be more effective than AI. Most people believe that the complexity and flexibility of human intelligence cannot be replicated by a computer. And your artificial intelligence is only as good as the information you, a human, give it.

## AVATAR

**AA vah tar • noun**

a cartoon-like character that represents the user in a game or virtual world

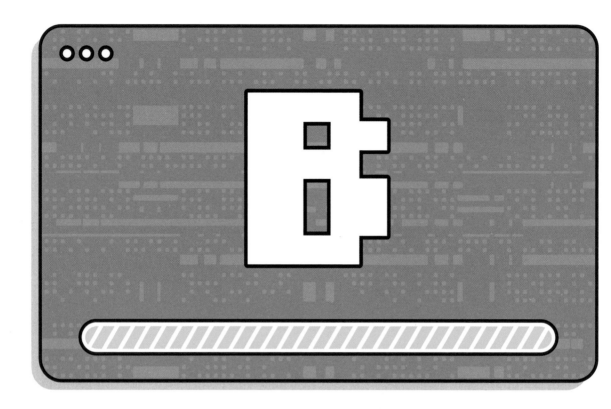

## BACKUP

**BAK uhp • noun**

a copy of a file that is stored in another location, like on an external hard drive

*When separated into two words, this term can be a verb, as in to "back up" your computer, or make a copy of its contents to store on the cloud or on an external drive.*

## BANDWIDTH

**BAND wihdth • noun**

the rate of transfer for data and information; how fast and how much data can be processed through a computer

## BCC

**BEE cee cee • noun or verb**

blind carbon copy, part of the email send field that hides the recipient's identity from other recipients

## BIG DATA

**bihg — DAY tah • noun**

a large amount of complex information, such as data collected by internet-connected devices

*If capitalized, Big Data means companies that have control over or access to users' information and that operate with the company's best interests in mind; for example Amazon or Facebook collect information about their users that can be used for targeting ads to those users.*

## BINARY CODE

**BYE nare ee — COHD • noun**

a way of writing numbers and data that uses only 0s and 1s

## BIOLOGICAL INTERFACE
bye oh LOH jick al — IHN tehr fayse • noun

a piece of technology that works between something biological and something digital (like from a muscle to a computer) and integrates the two

## BIOMETRIC DATA
bye oh MEH trik — DAY tah • noun

information about a person's physical characteristics, such as height, weight, fingerprints, voice, and DNA

## BIT
BIHT • noun

the smallest increment of data that can be measured in a computer

*A bit has a single binary value, meaning it has a value of 0 or 1. Eight bits make up 1 byte (see page 7).

## BLOCK
BLOK • verb

to ban a contact from communicating with you on social media or via text

## BLOCKCHAIN
BLOK chayn • noun

a system that records information in a decentralized way using digital ledgers (or records); each ledger is saved across the entire network so that it is very difficult to cheat or hack the system; each block is connected to the last block in the chain

## BLUE LIGHT
BLOO — LYTE • noun

a short, high-intensity wavelength of light visible to the human eye

*Like other colors of visible light, blue light is all around us. Computers or electronic devices that use light-emitting diode (LED) technology emit lots of blue light. Looking at those devices for a long time, especially after dark, may disrupt your sleep cycle.

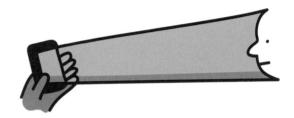

### Six Ways to Reduce the Effects of Blue Light

1. Cut down on screen time.
2. Take regular breaks from screens to rest your eyes. Looking away from your computer every 20 minutes is a good way to start.
3. Avoid blue light at night. Try to power down your devices at least 3 hours before bed.
4. Try on some new spectacles! Special glasses that filter out blue light can help lower your exposure and reduce eyestrain.
5. Add a screen filter to your smartphone, tablet, or computer.
6. Switch your devices to "night mode."

## BOOKMARK
### BOOK mahrk • verb

to save a web page's address in a browser; as a noun, a bookmark is sometimes called a "favorite"

## BOOLEAN EXPRESSION
### BOO lee ahn – ek SPRESH un • noun

a question that has only two possible answers, such as "true" and "false"

## BOOLEAN LOGIC
### BOO lee ahn – LAH jik • noun

a type of math for binary digits 0 (false) and 1 (true)

*Also called Boolean algebra, this math is named for its inventor, George Boole.*

## BOT
### BAHT • noun

a software program designed to automatically perform repetitive tasks on the internet; short for *robot* or *web robot* (see Good Bot, Bad Bot, right)

## BRANCH
### BRANCH • noun

a point in a program where two different options are available to choose from

# BROADBAND

**BRAWD band • noun**

the transmission of wide bandwidth data, voice, or video over long distances and at high speeds

# BROWSER

**BROW zur • noun**

a software program used to look at the internet; Safari, Firefox, and Chrome are popular browsers

*Sometimes called a web browser or internet browser.*

# BUG

**BUHG • noun**

a coding error in a computer program that can make a program break or behave in an unexpected way

# BYTE

**BYTE • noun**

a unit of measurement for digital information (see Byte Size, right)

## Byte Size

Computers have different units of measurement for data, to show how big something is. The most basic unit is a byte, which is made up of eight bits (that is, eight 0s or 1s).

Here are some bigger units of measurement:

**1 kilobyte (KB)**

contains roughly one thousand bytes (1,024 in binary, to be exact). A kilobyte could be a few paragraphs (less than a page) of text.

**1 megabyte (MB)**

contains about one million bytes. A megabyte could be a few minutes of music on an audio file.

**1 gigabyte (GB)**

contains roughly one billion bytes. A gigabyte could be a movie that plays on your TV.

**1 terabyte (TB)**

contains approximately one trillion bytes. A terabyte could be… 4.5 million e-books!

**1 petabyte (PB)**

contains one billion gigabytes. A petabyte could be enough storage for 20 million filing cabinets.

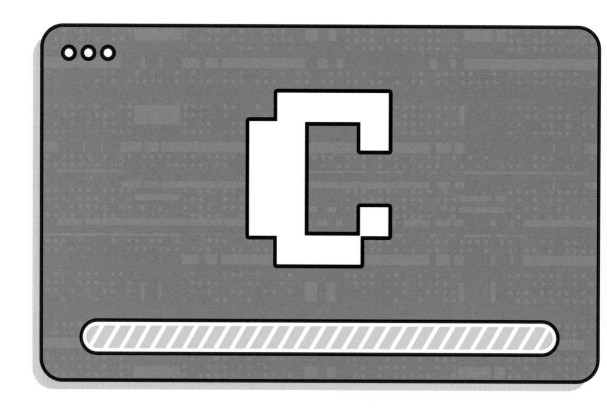

## CALL
**KAHL • verb**

to use a function in a program

## CAPS LOCK
**KAPS — lahk • noun**

a key on the keyboard that makes each letter that is typed a capital letter; caps lock is a toggle key, meaning it switches on when pressed and has to be pressed again to switch off

*\*HEY! Writing in all caps means THAT YOU'RE SHOUTING!*

## CARET
**CARE eht • noun**

a small up arrow that is often visible on the number 6 key on the keyboard (shift-6), also known as a "hat"; can also be a synonym for "cursor"

## CATFISH
**KAT fish • verb**

when someone pretends to be someone else online, usually through a fake profile or name on a social media website, with the purpose of deceiving a specific person (to make them emotionally compromised or upset, to make them give up money or other resources, or to provoke them)

## CC
**cee CEE • noun or verb**

part of the email send field, below "to"; a way of sending an email to someone who is not the direct recipient and that shares the recipient's identity with other recipients; short for *carbon copy* (see Real-Life Carbon Copies, opposite)

A B **C** D E F G H I J K L M N O P Q R S T U V W X Y Z

# CD / DVD / BLU-RAY DRIVE

**see DEE / dee vee DEE / BLUE-ray - DRYV • noun**

a machine that reads a CD, DVD, or Blu-ray disc and gives the computer access to the information on the disc

# CHAT ROOM

**CHAT - ROOM • noun**

a web page that allows users to talk to each other, usually about a specific topic; the precursor to modern-day messaging and communications platforms like Discord and Slack

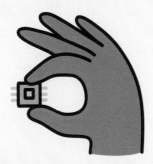

# CHIP

**CHIHP • noun**

a device made up of circuits and transistors that powers a computer's brain; made of semiconducting material, such as silicon

*Short for microchip, also referred to as a computer chip or integrated circuit*

# CIPHER

**SY phur • noun**

a coded message; also the key to a coded message

# CLICK

**KLIHK • verb**

the action of pressing the (left or only) mouse button, or tapping on a touch pad, to use the cursor on the computer screen

# CLICKBAIT

**KLIHK bayt • noun**

a headline that is written in a deceptive way that makes you want to read the article or story it links to but that may not be fully representative of the story or is promising more than the story can deliver

# CLOUD

**KLOWD • noun**

servers or a group of computers that provide a service like file storage or backup through the internet

## Real-Life Carbon Copies

Before email, when you sent a letter and wanted other people to get a copy of it, you would have used a thin tracing paper called carbon paper underneath the letter you were writing.

The pressure of the pen writing on the letter, or the typewriter keys hitting the page, would make the pigment transfer to the carbon paper below. That way, you could send an exact copy—a carbon copy—to someone who wasn't the direct recipient of the letter.

If you wanted the recipient to know who else would receive a copy of the letter, you'd write "CC" and the person's name. If you didn't, and you sent a copy to someone without calling it out in the letter, that would be a blind carbon copy (BCC).

9

## CODE

**COHD • *noun***

the symbols in a file or computer program that give instructions to the computer to tell it to do something; code is written in a programming language, such as Python, Ruby, PHP, Java, C++, Go, HTML, and many others

*Code can also be a verb when it's used to describe the process of writing code.*

## COMMAND

**kuh MAND • *noun***

a cue given to a computer by a user that tells it to do something

## COMPASSION FATIGUE

**kuhm PA shun – fuh TEEG • *noun***

when someone stops having a reaction to an event as a result of seeing it over and over, such as being bombarded by news on social media or TV or when a doctor internalizes stress from seeing many patients

*Emotional and physical exhaustion are common symptoms of compassion fatigue. It may mean that you have a harder time feeling the desire to help other people.*

## COMPILER

**kuhm PIE lur • *noun***

a program that takes a higher-level programming language like Java or C and translates it into lower-level instructions or machine code that the computer knows what to do with

## COMPRESSION

**kuhm PREH shun • *noun***

the process of making data a smaller size so that it takes up less space (also see *ZIP file*, page 53)

## COMPUTER

**kuhm PYOO ter • *noun***

an electronic device for working with information like numbers or words

## COMPUTER CASE

**kuhm PYOO ter – KAYSE • *noun***

the physical part of the computer that holds the other components

## COMPUTER SCIENCE

**kuhm PYOO ter – SY ense • *noun***

the study of computers and how they work

## CONSTANT

**KAHN stunt • *noun***

a value that is fixed and cannot change

## COOKIE

**COOK ee • *noun***

a small text file with information that can be passed back and forth between a web server and your browser

*Websites use cookies to track data and recognize specific users. Cookies save this information, such as your location, your login information, or the text size you prefer, to your web browser so that a server can read it. A login cookie is often set to expire after 24 hours so that you have to input the information again—it's a security precaution. Other cookies last longer.*

# CPU

see pee YEW • noun

stands for: **central processing unit**

the part of a computer that acts like the brain, sending electronic signals throughout the computer to tell it what to do, based on instructions coming from the software

# CRITICAL THINKING

KRI tick ul – THINK ing • noun

the process of using your senses, your brain, and what you already know to ask questions and think deeply about a subject, topic, or other information

# CRYPTOCURRENCY

KRIP toh kur rehn see • noun

money tokens that are digital files instead of physical currency; their value depends on what people are willing to pay for them, so it can fluctuate

*Sometimes abbreviated crypto, examples of cryptocurrency include Bitcoin, Ethereum, and Dogecoin. Cryptocurrency is not controlled by a centralized system like a bank. Instead, it is distributed by a decentralized technology called blockchain (see page 5).*

# CSS

see es ES • noun

stands for: **cascading style sheets**

a language used to show how elements on a web page are meant to be laid out, styled, and displayed; for example, you can use a file with one style sheet to create a look for an entire website

# CURSOR

KUR sir • noun

a small blinking line on the screen that shows where the next number or letter you type will go

# CUT AND PASTE

KUHT – AND – PAYST • verb

a basic computer operation that removes selected data, like text, and keeps it stored on a clipboard so it can be inserted somewhere else

*"Copy and paste" means you are making a copy of text and pasting it elsewhere, instead of moving it.*

# CYBER

SY ber • prefix or adjective

relating to the internet or computers

## DIG ⚙ DEEPER

### The Physical Cost of Virtual Coin

Even though cryptocurrency is a virtual currency and doesn't exist in physical form, like money... it does require mining!

Crypto mining is the process of creating individual blocks to add to the blockchain, and it uses up a ton of energy from electricity.

Mining rigs require computers that can quickly make complex computations to guess the correct solution to an equation.

If you have the fastest and best hardware and software, it can take about 10 minutes to mine one Bitcoin. If you are a home user, it could take up to 30 days!

# CYBERBULLYING

**SY ber buh lee ing • noun**

a serious form of online harassment that may include ridicule; stalking; posting hurtful, embarrassing, or inappropriate things about another person; sending unwanted emails or messages; spreading mean rumors; or anything to make another person feel sad, angry, or scared; cyberbullying can happen on the internet, on social media, or through texts, video games, apps, or other online forums

*Online bullying is a lot like in-person bullying. A bully's bad behavior is intentional and often repeated. See below for more on what to do if you encounter a bully online.*

# CYBERCRIME

**SY ber cryme • noun**

the act of committing criminal activities on computers or the internet, such as stealing someone's personal information or identity

# CYBERSECURITY

**SY ber sih kyur ih tee • noun**

the state of taking protective measures to try to protect your networks, computers, information, and other devices from attack

---

## DIG ⚙ DEEPER

### Be an Upstander

Bullies: Your classroom may have some or you might have learned what to do when you see one on the playground. Unfortunately, it can be even easier to bully someone online or using technology. Sometimes bullies stay anonymous, and other times they might be using text or social media with their name attached. Here are some tips for standing up to cyberbullies:

**What to do if you notice cyberbullying:**

- Don't participate in the bullying.
- Stand up for the person being bullied. This is called being an upstander! Tell the bully to stop and get other people to do the same.
- Report the situation to a trusted adult.

**What to do if you're the one being bullied:**

- Stop what you're doing and sign off immediately. It can be hard to ignore hurtful comments, but disconnecting and disengaging is your best course of action. Bullies get satisfaction from reactions. Don't respond, and get out of there.
- Block them! Stay away from places where the person hangs out online. But save the evidence of bullying—take screenshots or pictures. Report the incident if you're on an app with rules about community behavior.
- Talk to a safe friend. They can help you remember that you're not alone, that it's not your fault, and that you're amazing.
- Acknowledge your own feelings. Even though bullying behavior is a reflection of the bully, not you, it can still be hurtful.
- Tell a trusted adult, someone you can count on.

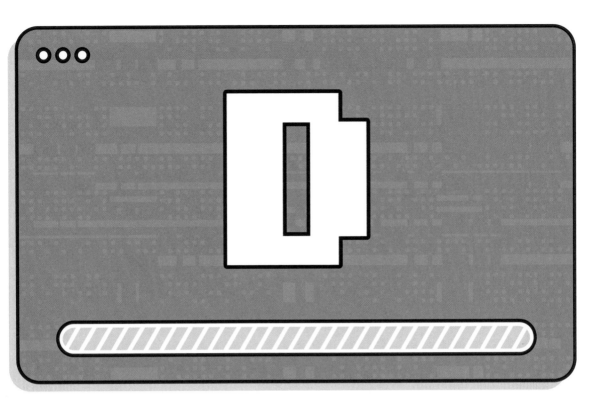

## DARK WEB
**DARK - WEHB • noun**

content on the internet that can only be accessed by a special search engine, run by a specific browser software called Tor ("The Onion Routing" project)

*On the dark web, there's no visibility into who has set up a website or who is accessing it because the network encrypts requests and makes it hard to track them. This allows users to be anonymous.*

## DATA
**DAY tuh or DA tuh • noun**

information, facts, or statistics that have been stored on a computer

## DATABASE
**DAY tuh bayse or DA tuh bayse • noun**

any organized collection of information, or data, usually stored in a computer system and searchable via computer

## DATA COMPRESSION
**DAY tuh - kum PREH shun • noun**

the process of reducing the size of your data so that it can have a smaller file size

*The number of bits needed to store the data is smaller in a compressed file. To restore the file to its original form, you need to decompress it.*

## DEBUG
**dee BUHG • verb**

to go through a program that isn't working, look for mistakes, and correct them; or to run a program that helps you look for mistakes in another program

# DEEPFAKE

**DEEP fayke • noun**

an image, video, or audio file that has been altered to change someone's face, body, or voice to make it look like they said or did something they didn't say or do (see That's Unreal!, right)

# DESKTOP

**DESK tahp • noun**

the home display of a computer screen that shows the recycling bin and other files or shortcuts to favorite programs

*The word* desktop, *as in desktop computer, can also refer to a personal computer that's not a laptop.*

# DIGITAL

**DIH jeh tul • adjective**

having to do with, relating to, or using electronic technologies, tools, or devices that can store, send, or receive information through numbers

# DIGITAL CITIZENSHIP

**DIH jeh tul – SIT ih zen ship • noun**

the idea of using the internet and other technology in a responsible, appropriate, safe, and effective way

# DIGITAL DIVIDE

**DIH jeh tul – dih VYDE • noun**

the gap between people who have access to computers, the internet, and other electronic devices, and people who do not and cannot benefit from them (see Digital Equality for All!, opposite)

# DIGITAL IDENTITY

**DIH jeh tul – eye DEN tih tee • noun**

all of the information that's present online about an individual, organization, or electronic device

## DIG ⚙ DEEPER

### That's Unreal!

Making a deepfake video is getting easier as technology develops. Deepfake creators can manipulate videos that already exist or manufacture new videos using a combination of images and video.

The problem is that it's becoming harder to trust what you see! A deepfake could be used to trick the public into believing that a celebrity has endorsed a particular product or brand or that a world leader has said something he or she never said.

Some scientists, like Dr. Wael AbdAlmageed at the University of Southern California, are developing methods to test whether a video is a deepfake. These tests look for small defects in the video that the human eye cannot see. Dr. AbdAlmageed recommends researching a video before believing that what you see is true and slowing it down to look for inconsistencies.

# DIGITAL LITERACY

**DIH jeh tul – LIH teh rah see • noun**

the ability to understand how technology is used, including how to search for, evaluate, and create information using technology, and understanding what its limitations and dangers are

# DIRECTORY

**dih RECK toh ree • noun**

a place where files can be stored and organized

## DOMAIN

**doh MAYN • noun**

part of the internet that is made up of a series of computers or websites that are similar in function or purpose; they share the same abbreviation, like .org for advocacy websites or nonprofits, .edu for websites of higher education, and .gov for government websites

## DOOMSCROLL

**DOOM skrohl • verb**

to mindlessly flick through a feed, especially on social media, and especially if the feed is full of scary, depressing, or sad news stories

## DOS ATTACK

**DOSS – uh TACK • noun**

stands for: **denial of service attack**

when data is sent to a computer with the goal of overwhelming the computer and stopping it from doing its tasks

## DOUBLE-CLICK

**duh buhl–KLIHK • verb**

the process of clicking a mouse button two times quickly in succession; double-clicking will open a program and is used to make a selection or interact with a program or document on a computer

*On a touchscreen or trackpad, this action has the same function but is called a double-tap.*

## DOWNLOAD

**DOWN lohd • noun or verb**

refers to data being retrieved from a source and copied to your computer

## DRAG AND DROP

**DRAG–AND–DRAHP • verb**

a method of moving an object onscreen from one place to another, using the mouse

*To drag and drop: Click on one object, hold, drag it onscreen to its new location, then release.*

## DRIVER

**DRY vur • noun**

a set of files or a piece of code that tells hardware (like a printer) how to work with the operating system

---

### Digital Equality for All!

More than half of the world's population does not have access to the internet. The digital divide unfairly affects certain groups of people more than others—such as people who can't afford internet access or don't live near high-speed cable networks.

**How is life harder without the internet? Here are a few examples:**

- You can't apply to jobs online.
- Doing research for homework or turning in homework online is impossible.
- You can't schedule appointments for healthcare online.
- Working or attending school from home or taking video meetings on the computer is a no-go.
- Students are more likely to miss out on up-to-date information and access to resources that their peers with internet access would be able to get at home.

# A Few Folks Who Changed Computer Science History

## 1  Early Calculations

**Ada Lovelace** was the only child of a poet and a mathematician. As a teenager, her aptitude for math—a subject that she had studied intensively from a young age, thanks to her mother—began to blossom. Ada met inventor, mathematician, and philosopher **Charles Babbage** at a party when she was 17 years old, and they began a correspondence.

Eventually Babbage, who gave Ada the nickname "Enchantress of Numbers," began creating an early computer called an analytical engine. As Ada learned about this new machine, she was eager to help him promote it. She recognized that this computer could have applications beyond solving math problems and calculations, and she is credited with publishing the first computer algorithm.

Because of this achievement, she has gone down in history as the first computer pro-grammer—even though no programming languages had been invented yet when she was alive.

## 2  Computing and Code-Breaking

**Alan Turing**, a British mathematician who served his country during World War II, had the top secret job of code breaker, de-crypting messages created by the Enigma machine, a device that Germany and its allies were using to send information across enemy lines. The machine used a cipher that the Germans would change daily, which made their communications even harder to decode.

Although the code created by the Enigma machine was thought to be unbreakable, Turing cracked it. His many achievements are widely taught today, but Turing was not aware of the impact his work had on the world during his lifetime.

## 3  A Language Artist

US Navy rear admiral and programming pioneer **Grace Murray Hopper** was one of the first programmers of the Harvard Mark I computer, an electromechanical calculator used in World War II. She helped develop UNIVAC, the first all-electronic digital computer, and coined many terms related to computing, such as "bug" to mean a glitch in a computer's functioning.

"Amazing Grace" also had the idea to write computer programs in English and word-based languages rather than just numbers and symbols, paving the way for the programming languages that are essential to modern computing. She correctly predicted that computers would someday be small enough for everyone to use and that they would be part of the lives of everyday people, not just scientists.

 ## 4 The ENIAC Programmers

In 1946, six women—**Kay McNulty**, **Betty Jean Jennings**, **Betty Snyder**, **Marlyn Wescoff**, **Frances Bilas**, and **Ruth Lichterman**—programmed a computer called ENIAC, which stands for Electronic Numerical Integrator and Computer. It was a machine that could store information—the first of its kind—and was made up of 18,000 vacuum tubes and 40 panels that were eight feet tall.

They used no programming languages or tools, but instead had to maneuver the machine's many switches and cables to program the machine. Despite their creative and innovative work, their identities were not revealed to the public after ENIAC was announced to the world and the press.

 ## 5 NASA Before Computers

**Katherine Johnson**, the first African American woman to graduate from West Virginia University, was a physicist and scientist for NASA in a time when women, and especially women of color, were almost unheard of as top scientists. She came to NASA to work under another remarkable

woman, **Dorothy Vaughan**, who was the first African American manager of the Langley Research Center and a competent rocket scientist herself.

Johnson is best known for her mathematical calculations that allowed other people to explore space. She plotted the trajectory of the first human spaceflight in 1961 and then went on to calculate John Glenn's orbit of Earth and also the Apollo 11—the first manned mission to the moon.

She died in February of 2020, having been honored with a research center dedicated to her at NASA and a movie called *Hidden Figures*, which tells the story of her by-hand calculations of the flight of Apollo 11.

 ## 6 Unsung Software Creators

**Dennis Ritchie**, creator of the C programming language—the mother of all programming languages—changed the way people use and think about computers and computer science. Using C, he and **Ken Thompson** cocreated the operating systems family called Unix while they were at AT&T's Bell Labs.

A derivative of Unix is the foundation for all of Apple's current operating systems. Unix is also the reason that most software is open-source today (see page 31). Ironically, Ritchie's death in 2011 was largely overshadowed by the passing of Steve Jobs, the cofounder of Apple, whose products wouldn't be possible without Ritchie's innovations.

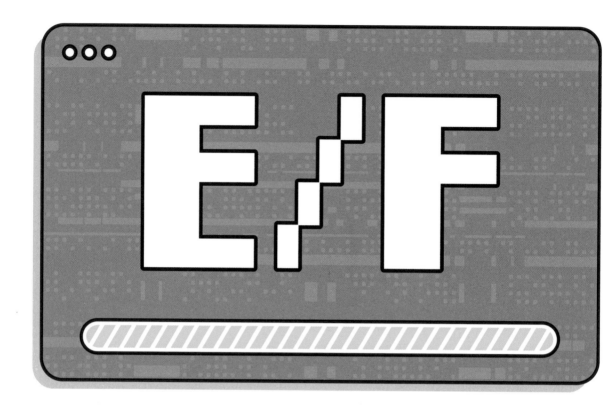

## ELECTRONIC FOOTPRINT

e lek TRON ik – FOOT print • noun

a record of all the online activity by a person on the internet

## EMAIL

EE mail • noun

a message that may contain text, files, images, or attachments; emails are sent through a network, or over the internet, from one person to another

## ENCODE

en COHD • verb

to convert information or an instruction into a secret coded format so that a computer can understand it; for example, used to describe software encryption

## ENCRYPTION

en KRIP shun • noun

the process of converting information into a code or a coded message so that only the intended people can read it

## ENTER KEY

EN tur – KEE • noun

the key on a keyboard that lets the computer know to run a command that has just been typed; also known as a return key

## EVENT

uh VENT • noun

an action that a computer takes in reaction to an external cue, such as a key being pressed

## EXTERNAL HARD DRIVE

ECKS tur nul – HARD – DRYV • noun phrase

a device with storage space that can be plugged into a computer through a port

## FACIAL RECOGNITION SOFTWARE

FAY shul – reh kug NIH shun – SAWFT ware • noun phrase

a type of computer program that identifies faces using an algorithm (see Facial Recognition—or Not, page 20)

## FEED

FEED • noun

a news reel that you can scroll through

## FIBER

FYE bur • noun

a connection that uses pulses of light to move data from one place to another; short for *fiber optics, fiber-optic internet,* or *fiber-optic cables*

## FILE

FYL • noun

a resource for recording and storing information in a computer; a common unit of storage that can be named

## FILE EXTENSION

FYL – eck STEN shun • noun

the letters that come after the period in a file name that tell the computer what kind of software to use with it

*Can also be called a file name extension.*

## FILE SHARING

FYL – SHARE ing • noun

the ability to grant access to the same file to multiple users

## FIREWALL

FYRE wohl • noun

a security system (software or hardware) that monitors information going in and out of a computer or network, creating a barrier or blocking activity based on safety rules it has been given

*An administrator could set up a firewall to keep a user from visiting a particular website, like a gaming website, or to keep traffic from suspicious sources from getting into a network.*

## FIRMWARE
### FURM ware • noun

a type of software program that is written permanently into a hardware device

## FLOAT
### FLOAT • noun

a number that has a decimal point; can be more precise than an integer (see page 25)

## FORUM
### FOR uhm • noun

an area where a group can have an online discussion

## FUNCTION
### FUNK shun • noun

a specific formula or section of a program that does part of a larger task or routine

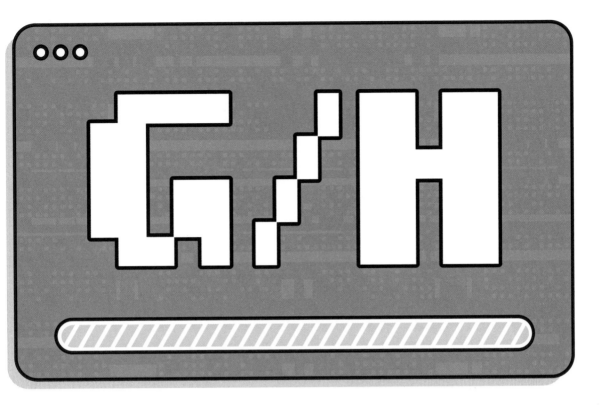

## GATE

**GAYT • noun**

a gate, or a logic gate, is a series of signals that help computers make decisions based on a rule; there are three basic types of gates: "AND," "OR," and "NOT"

## GEEK

**GEEK • noun**

an informal word for someone who is enthusiastic and excitable about a certain topic or group of related topics

## GEOFENCING

**JEE OH fehn sing • verb**

setting up a geographic boundary virtually (on an app, for example) and tracking when a device moves in or out of it

*For example, an art gallery might set up a geofence and send ads to specifically target people whose phones are located in a five-mile radius of the gallery.*

## GLITCH

**GLICH • noun**

a small snag or a minor operating failure; also a spike in voltage to an electrical circuit

## GPU

**gee pee YEW • noun**

stands for: **graphics processing unit**

a processor that allows images to be displayed on a computer screen

A B C D E F (G  H) I J K L M N O P Q R S T U V W X Y Z

## GRAPHICS
**GRA fix • *noun***

any visual elements displayed on a computer that are not text, such as art, images, icons, or symbols

## GUI
**gee yew EYE • *noun***

stands for: **graphical user interface**

the buttons and windows that make up the part of the program you can see and interact with

## HACKER
**HAK ur • *noun***

a person who breaks into a computer system; anyone who makes a piece of technology do something it isn't supposed to do, like grant access to password-protected content without a password (see What Color Is Your Hacker Hat?, right)

## HARD DRIVE
**HARD – DRYV • *noun***

a storage device that can be used to store data; also called a *hard disk drive*

## HARDWARE
**HARD ware • *noun***

any of the parts of a computer that can be physically touched or seen, like the keyboard, the motherboard, the fans, and so on

## HASHING
**HASH ing • *verb***

the act of making a string of characters into a key that represents the original

*Hash is also the word for a pound sign. That's where we get the name hashtag, for a keyword tag on social media like #NoFilter.*

### What Color Is Your Hacker Hat?

A hacker is...not exclusively a bad guy! There are actually three types of hackers, and they're known as:

- **White hat:** Someone whose job it is to figure out where security systems are vulnerable; this person uses their hacking skills for the good of an organization.

- **Black hat:** Typically what you think when you think "hacker"; this person is looking to harm people, companies, or websites, or make a profit.

- **Grey hat:** This type of hacker is somewhere in between black and white. They may intend no harm with their hacks or claim that their mission is to make the internet a safer or better place, like an online Robin Hood. However, that doesn't mean that what they're doing is legal or ethical.

## HEURISTIC
**HYU ris tik • *noun***

a method for solving a problem quickly (as opposed to thoroughly)

## HEXADECIMAL
**HECKS uh dess ih mul • *noun***

a number system based on the number 16, where the numbers 10, 11, 12, 13, 14, and 15 are represented by the letters A, B, C, D, E, and F

## HOME KEYS

**HOHM – KEEZ • noun**

the keys where your fingers should rest on the keyboard: *asdf jkl;* on the QWERTY keyboard (see pages 38 and 39)

## HOMEPAGE

**hohm PAYGE • noun**

the main page of a website that usually leads you to all the other pages on the site

*\*Landing page, welcome page, or front page can all be synonyms (words that mean the same thing) of homepage.*

## HONEYPOT

**HUHN ee paht • noun**

a vulnerable computer system that you set up to lure cybercriminals, to study who is attacking you, and to learn how you can defend against them

## HTML

**aych tee em EL • noun**

stands for: **HyperText Markup Language**

the language web pages are built in; used to display data, such as describing the structure of a web page and displaying information on that page

## HTTP

**aych tee tee PEE • noun**

stands for: **HyperText Transfer Protocol**

the set of standards and procedures for data transfer on the world wide web

## HUB

**HUHB • noun**

the central part of a network

## HYPERLINK

**HI pur link • noun**

a photo, icon, or text that takes you to another page or file when you click it; also known as a *web link*, or simply a *link*

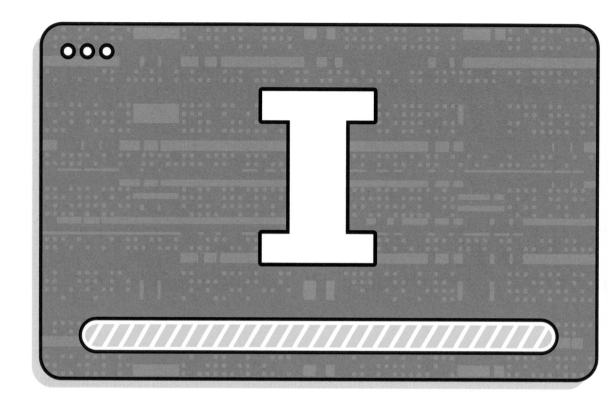

## ICON
### EYE kahn • noun

a graphic on the screen that represents a program, application, or file

## IF-ELSE STATEMENT
### IF – ELSE – STAYT mehnt • noun

a piece of code that will do one thing if the if statement is proved true and another thing if the if statement is false

*For example, IF the sky is blue, fly a kite... ELSE go back inside. (The "else" usually is the opposite of what was in your if statement.)*

## IF STATEMENT
### IF – STAYT mehnt • noun

a piece of code that will do something when the if statement is proved true

*For example, "IF the sky is blue, then go fly a kite." These statements can vary—some programming languages use "if-then."*

## INPUT
### IHN put • noun

any information that is put into, given to, or taken into a computer or device

*A microphone, for example, takes in audio data.*

## INSTANT MESSAGING
### IHN stunt – MESS uh jing • noun

a direct form of communication between two people over a network or the internet; also known as IM or DM, for *direct messaging*

## INTEGER

IN tuh jer • noun

a whole number (not a fraction) that does not have a decimal point

## INTELLECTUAL PROPERTY

ihn teh LEK shu al – PRAH pur tee • noun

a work or a creation that is not a physical object but that has value and can belong to someone, such as an idea, a formula, or a poem; it can be protected by a copyright or patent

## INTERFACE

IHN tur fayse • noun

the means by which the user interacts with software or hardware

## INTERNET

IHN tur net • noun

a global network of computers that are connected to other computers; provides information and communication

## INTERNET OF THINGS

IN tur net – OF – THINGS • noun

a name for all the different devices that have computers in them and are connected to the internet, such as smart light switches

## INTERPRETER

ihn TER preh tur • noun

a program that translates code or instructions into machine code (see also From Letters to Numbers, page 47)

## IP ADDRESS

eye PEE – uh DRES • noun

stands for: **internet protocol address**

a label that is made up of numbers and is unique to a computer when it is connected to the internet

## ISP

eye ess PEE • noun

stands for: **internet service provider**

a company that provides internet access to customers through a network service

## ITERATE

IT ur ate • verb

to repeat a sequence of instructions

*An iteration is the process of repeating a function or a sequence of instructions.*

## JPEG

**JAY peg • *noun***

a format for a compressed image file; extension ending in .jpg (see also *data compression* page 13)

## KEY

**KEE • *noun***

in cryptography, a string of characters used to lock or unlock a message

## KEYBOARD

**KEE bord • *noun***

hardware that allows you to interact with a computer; made up of letters, numbers, symbols, and words

## KEYCAP

**KEE cahp • *noun***

the cover that sits on top of the switch on a keyboard; each keycap has a letter, symbol, or word on it

## KEYLOGGER

**KEE lah ger • *noun***

a program that can record which keys you are pressing in order to figure out your passwords or other sensitive information

## KEYWORD

**KEE werd • *noun***

a word or a phrase that can help return results in a search

## LANGUAGE

**LAN gwij • *noun***

a vocabulary and set of rules that can give instructions to and communicate with a computer

A  B  C  D  E  F  G  H  I  J  K  L  M  N  O  P  Q  R  S  T  U  V  W  X  Y  Z

## LAPTOP

**LAHP tohp • noun**

a portable computer, also known as a notebook, that is designed to be small and fit in a lap; typically shaped like a rectangle, able to be opened, with a display, a keyboard, and a trackpad

## LATENCY

**LAY ten see • noun**

the amount of time it takes for data to get from one physical point to another

## LCD

**ell cee DEE • noun**

stands for: **liquid crystal display**

a type of monitor that uses LEDs (see next definition)

## LED

**ell ee DEE • noun**

stands for: **light-emitting diode**

a type of light used in a monitor screen

## LEFT-CLICK

**LEHFT–KLIHK • verb**

see *click* page 9

*The left-click button of a mouse is usually the main button that a user works with to complete tasks on a computer; it's called left-click because sometimes the mouse has a right-click button.*

## LIBRARY

**LYE breh ree • noun**

a collection of resources or functions that can be used in multiple projects

## LOG OFF

**LAHG – OFF • verb**

to sign out or end a session as a particular user; logging back in will usually require a password

## LOG ON

**LAHG – ON • verb**

signing in to use a system, software, or program; usually requires a password

## LOOP

**LEWP • noun**

a program that repeats itself or that can repeat a task under a circumstance

### Become Multilingual!

There are so many programming languages, it can be hard to know where to start if you want to learn to code. Just a handful of the most popular languages are listed below. The names in bold are the best for beginners.

| | | |
|---|---|---|
| Ada | Fortran | R |
| **Alice** | Go | **Ruby** |
| BASIC | Java | Rust |
| **Blockly** | JavaScript | **Scratch** |
| C | Lua | Swift |
| C++ | Perl | Visual Basic |
| C# | PHP | |
| COBOL | **Python** | |

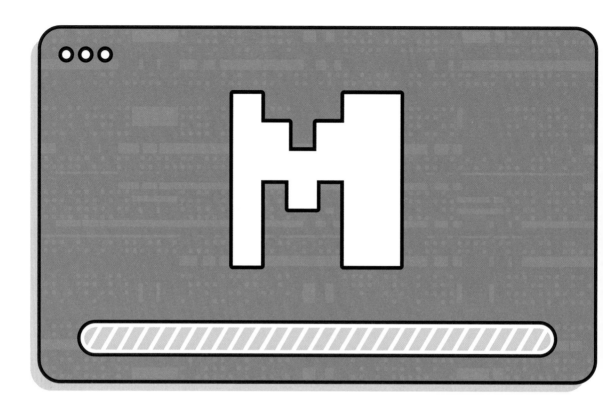

## MACHINE CODE

### muh SHEEN – KOHD • noun

the most basic language that a computer can understand; uses binary code or hexadecimal (see page 22) instructions

*Programming languages have to be translated into machine code so that the computer can read the instructions in its own language.*

## MACHINE LEARNING

### muh SHEEN – LUHR ning • noun

a science that focuses on teaching a computer how to learn to do something on its own, imitating the way humans learn, rather than programming it to do something

## MALWARE

### MAAL wear • noun

software that is designed with the intent to cause malice and dysfunction, such as spying on someone or causing errors in a device

*Malware is a shorter way to say "malicious software."*

## MEME

### MEEHM • noun

a funny, interesting, or delightful idea, text, image, or video that spreads quickly through the internet

## MEMORY

### MEHM oh ree • noun

the area where a computer stores data or instructions

## METADATA

**meh tuh DAY tuh • noun**

data that gives descriptive information about other data; for example, the size of an image file

## METAVERSE

**MEH tuh vuhrse • noun**

a space where you can live a second life online and interact with other people in a computer-generated environment or virtual reality

## MIXED REALITY

**MIXT – ree AL ih tee • noun**

the combination of elements of augmented reality (see page 3) and virtual reality (page 50), in which real-world objects and digital objects can interact

## MOBILE

**MOH bul • adjective**

the ability to be moved; can describe a phone

## MODEM

**MOH dehm • noun**

a hardware device that helps a computer or router (see page 40) connect to the internet

## MODULE

**MAH (d)juul • noun**

a distinct section of code that performs a single part of an overall program and can be independently distributed

## MONITOR

**MOHN ih ter • noun**

an output device that displays visuals on a screen and can connect to your computer so you can view the desktop

## MOORE'S LAW

**MORZ – LAW • noun**

the idea that the number of transistors (see page 46) you can fit on a computer chip, or its processing power, will double every 18 months to two years, especially when compared to size and cost

*Moore's law may become obsolete soon, even though it's held up for roughly 50 years! Transistor size is determined by the laws of physics.*

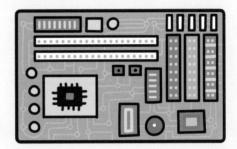

## MOTHERBOARD

**MUH thur bord • noun**

the central circuit board of a computer; the motherboard holds and connects the CPU, memory, and other important parts of the hardware

## MOUSE

**MAUS • noun**

a handheld device that is used to control the cursor to select text, icons, files, or folders; sometimes it has buttons for a left- and a right-click (or just one button, for left-click)

## MULTITASK

**MUHL tee task • verb**

to have multiple applications running at the same time

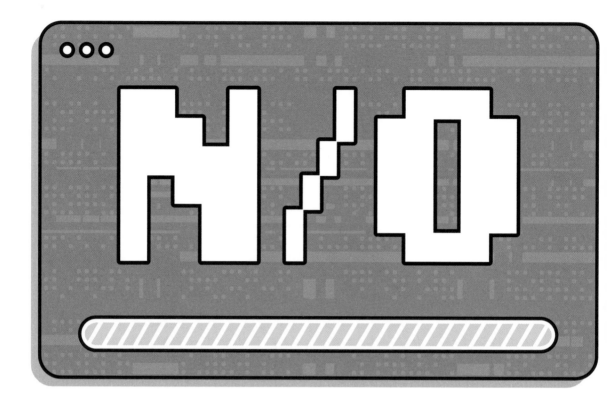

## NET NEUTRALITY

**NEHT – new TRAH lih tee • noun**

the idea that the internet should be free and that service providers should not block anyone from accessing any part of its content or services (see Net Equity, right)

## NETWORK

**NEHT werk • noun**

a system of two or more computers that are connected and can share data and resources

## NFT

**enn eff TEE • noun**

stands for: **non-fungible token**

a unique unit of data, or token, that can be owned by a person and cannot be duplicated; NFTs can represent any kind of digital file, like a piece of graphic art or a song (see Fungi-what?, opposite)

### DIG ⚙ DEEPER

### Net Equity

The concept of net neutrality is essential to being able to navigate the internet freely. Without it, companies that provide access to the internet can...

- slow down your internet access speeds when they want to

- block certain websites they don't want you to be able to visit

- put applications or services behind a paywall (see page 33)

- make you use a certain search engine that they prefer

- or make it so that people who can pay for information are the only ones who can access it

## ONLINE

*ahn LYNE • adjective*

a term that refers to something that is connected to the internet, a network, or a computer

## ONLINE IDENTITY

*ahn LYNE – eye DEN tih tee • noun*

the self (or selves) that a user presents to the internet or the digital world

## OPEN-SOURCE

*OH pun-SORHSE • adjective*

describes a type of software where the source code is available to be looked at or viewed publicly through a license

*\*A license defines what you can and can't do with the code: Some licenses allow you to do whatever you want, while other licenses are more restrictive and might require you to make your version open-source or won't allow you to use it commercially (see Free vs. Open-Source Software, page 32).*

*In closed-source software (like Windows software), no one can see the code behind the software.*

---

### DIG ⚙ DEEPER

## Fungi-what?

Even though they have *fungi* in their names, fungible and non-fungible tokens have nothing to do with mushrooms. They have to do with uniqueness.

For example: Currency, or money, is fungible. This means that a dollar that your friend has in their possession is equal in value to and could be replaced by a dollar that you have.

However, a watercolor painting that you made in kindergarten is non-fungible. It is one of a kind, and you can't make another one.

NFTs use blockchain (see page 5) to record the ownership of a piece of unique art. Because blockchain provides a transparent record, anyone can look up an NFT's history to see if anyone else has ever owned it. If you own an NFT, you own the only one of its kind. Anything else that looks like it is just a copy.

## NODE

**NOHD • noun**

a device or a data point that sends or receives communication through a network

## ONE

**WUHN • noun**

a number used to represent "true" to a computer

## OPERATOR

**AH pur ay ter • noun**

a symbol that performs a specific function

## OS

**oh ESS • noun**

stands for: **Operating System**

the main program or software that a computer uses to connect the hardware to the software and to run other programs (see below for examples)

## OUTPUT

**OUT puht • noun**

data that is created by a computer or program and is viewed or heard on an output device like a screen, speaker, or printer

### Free vs. Open-Source Software

Open-source and free might sound like the same thing, but they are quite different.

The messaging app Signal is both free and open-source, meaning that anyone can use it for no cost, but anyone can also look at the source code to see what the application is doing. To find out if it's giving away your information or data to a company, or to find out anything else you'd like to know about the way it works, you can just check the source code.

It's kind of like if someone gave you a free cake (free) vs. if someone gave you the recipe for the cake (open-source). If someone gave you a cake for free, you could enjoy it, but you wouldn't know first-hand what's in it. If you got the recipe, you could make the cake yourself and you'd know exactly what you put in it because you did the baking.

### The Software That You Need to Use Other Software

The first computers didn't have operating systems, and as a result, they could do only one thing at a time. Modern operating systems allow you to multitask—to listen to music while you play video games or scroll through social media. They work behind the scenes to tell the computer hardware what to do. They are responsible for managing the computer's memory and the user interface, for talking to input and output devices, and for running software and programs.

Here are some examples of operating systems:

- **Unix:** an operating system that is the basis of many others today

- **Linux:** an operating system with a penguin mascot

- **macOS:** Apple's operating system

- **Windows:** created by Microsoft, Bill Gates's company, this OS is used by a majority of desktop and laptop computers

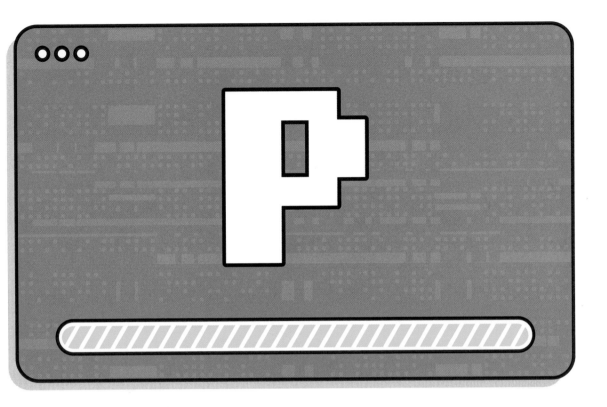

## PACKET

**PAA kit • noun**

a small package of data that is sent over a network

## PASSWORD

**PAS wurd • noun**

a private, secret set of numbers, letters, and/or symbols that a user inputs with a username to log into a program

## PATTERN RECOGNITION

**PAH turn – reh kog NI shun • noun**

the process of seeing similarities or predictable repetitions so that a computer can solve problems more easily

## PAYWALL

**PAY wohl • noun**

a barrier to entry that requires payment, such as on a website that charges money for its services or information

### 1234...Password!

Passwords should be strong to make sure they can't be cracked.

How do you make a strong password? Here are five tips:

1. Use capital letters, numbers, and symbols in your password.

2. Make your password more than eight characters (when possible since some websites limit you to a character amount).

3. Use a sentence or phrase instead of a single word, like: #IamaMarioKartchamp10n

4. Don't use words that are easy to guess, like your street address, hometown, or birthday.

5. Even better...use a password manager that comes up with hard-to-crack passwords!

## PC

**pee SEE • noun**

stands for: **personal computer**

a computer that is for general use at home by an individual

## PCB

**pee see BEE • noun**

stands for: **printed circuit board**

a thin piece of fiberglass that acts as a circuit; components like chips can be connected to it and assembled to form a working electronic device

## PERIPHERAL

**peh RIFF er al • noun**

a device or piece of hardware that can provide input and output for a computer

## PHISHING

**FIH shing • noun**

fake web pages or emails that are designed to look trustworthy to get people to reveal their personal information to cybercriminals

## PHOTOSHOP

**FOH toh shohp • verb**

to change a digital image to make it look different (such as, using art tools to change grey hair to brown hair or to remove a person from the background); named after software called Adobe Photoshop

## PING

**PING • verb**

to send a request to a website or host that asks for a response

## PIXEL

**PIK sul • noun**

the most basic unit of color on a display or in an image; on a screen, a pixel appears as one of the tiny squares or dots that make up the larger picture; short for *picture elements*

## PLUG-IN

**PLUHG–ihn • noun**

software that enhances a host program and adds new functions to it without changing what it can already do, such as an internet browser plug-in that saves and recalls your passwords and login information

## PORT

**PORT • noun**

an interface where hardware can be plugged into a device

## POWER SUPPLY

**POW er – suh PLY • noun**

a device that adapts the power from the electric socket in the wall into power that the insides of the computer can use

## PRINTER

**PRIHN tur • noun**

an external hardware device that uses ink to print image or text files onto a piece of paper

*3D printers create a three-dimensional object! They use plastic or powdery metal inks.*

## Why Is Privacy Important Online?

You might not think that internet privacy is a big deal—after all, who cares what videos you're watching or what articles you're reading (besides your parents or guardians)? But it's important to protect yourself and your personal information.

First: Revealing your location, birthday, phone number, your pet's name, or even your face can give people who aren't your friends access to information that can be misused to steal your identity or put you in danger.

Second: Even if you never give out any personal details, information about you is still being tracked and logged no matter what you do online.

For example, some companies use cookies (see page 10) to track your movements around the internet.

Cookies can tell them how long you stay on a webpage, or if you interact with it—like if you added something to an online cart.

Companies use this information on their own websites. For example, they can give you more targeted advertisements for products they think you'll like. But they are also building a profile of your interests and all of your online activities and history. This personal profile can be sold to other companies…so you never know what might happen with that information or who might end up with it.

**Remember that anything you share to the internet is on the internet... permanently!**

# PRIVACY
**PREYE vuh see • noun**

the right that all people have to keep their personal information to themselves and control how it is used (see Why Is Privacy Important Online?, left)

*This type of privacy is known as data privacy.*

# PROCESSOR
**PROH sess ohr • noun**

an electronic chip inside a computer that follows instructions

# PROGRAM
**PROH grahm • noun**

instructions written in code that a computer uses to complete a task

# PROGRAMMING
**PROH grahm ing • noun**

the process of writing code to instruct a computer to do something

# PROTOCOL
**PROH tuh kol • noun**

a set of rules that allows different devices to talk to each other and exchange data

# The Pros and Cons of Social Media

Social media has changed the way we connect and learn and even how we see ourselves. This can be a double-edged sword: Although social media can benefit our lives, it can also come with some problems.

## Impact on Relationships

**PROS:**

- Social media can help to create intimacy with friends and improve connections with your community.

- It may be easier to connect or grow friendships on social media for someone who identifies as shy.

- Social media is useful for keeping in touch with family and friends who live far away and for allowing groups or individuals to communicate en masse.

**CONS:**

- Social media can harm connections with others. Bullying, threats, and an atmosphere of criticism and negativity can occur during social media interactions. Sometimes interacting through a screen can dehumanize the person on the other end, making it seem like they're not a real human being with feelings.

- People have reported a feeling of disconnection associated with relationships on social media.

- It is easy to feel rejected when social media posts don't receive the feedback we wanted or expected. Some people feel frustrated, lonely, or paranoid about being left out.

- The anonymity of social media can be part of the problem.

## Stay Safe on Social

There are many ways to keep yourself safe online. Here are three tips:

1. Set your social media accounts to PRIVATE MODE so you can decide who can see and read your posts. Keep your posts private so that your location or information can only be seen by followers of your choosing.

2. Do not add people you don't know on social media accounts.

3. Never post personal information on public posts, such as your address, age, or any other identifying information.

## Good to Know

The term "social network" refers both to a person's connections to other people in the real world and to a platform that supports online communication, such as Instagram, TikTok, Snapchat, Facebook, or Twitter.

## Impact on Identity

**PROS:**

- Social media can help people to express their true identities.

- Social media allows you to write and edit your thoughts and use images to express yourself. This vulnerability and exposure can be very powerful in letting other people in and making them feel a part of your life.

**CONS:**

- Social media can lead to inauthentic representations of some people. Seeing others' carefully curated posts and perfect-seeming feeds can amplify feelings of loneliness or low self-esteem. The photos people post to social media are often not representative of the full picture of their lives—but it can be easy to forget that and end up in a cycle of comparison or shame.

- It is easy to feel suspicious of the way others use photo editing to disguise their identities or situations.

- Many people feel self-conscious about posting selfies or other images of themselves and worry that the feedback they might receive would affect their feelings of self-worth.

## Be Authentic and Smart

1. **Be your own self.** Don't pretend to be someone else or comment anonymously.

2. **Be nice.** Don't hide behind the screen to say or post mean things. Don't be a troll.

3. **Be real.** Don't say or post things about someone that you would not say face-to-face.

4. **Be smart about what you post.** Remember that once you post something, it is out there for anyone to see.

5. **Be a real friend.** Never send inappropriate pictures of someone to your friends.

6. **Be smart, really smart.** Never, ever engage in sexual conversations with peers or strangers online. Never send inappropriate pictures of yourself or ask for inappropriate pictures of anybody. Never send passwords or other personal identification information to anyone.

## The Numbers

More than **90 percent** of teenagers in the United States have a smartphone.

Teenagers ages 13–18 spend about **9 hours daily** on entertainment media, including social media and media like TV, online videos, reading, and mobile games; **90 percent** of kids in this age group have used social media, and **75 percent** say they have at least one active account.

Tweens ages 8–12 average about **6 hours per day** online.

**Sixty-five percent** of parents say they worry about the amount of time their kids spend online.

## QR CODE

**kew AR – COHD • *noun***

stands for: **Quick Response code**

a barcode of black and white squares that stores data that machines, like the camera on your phone, can read

## QUANTUM COMPUTER

**KWAN *tuhm* – *kuhm* PYOO *ter* • *noun***

a really fast computer that uses subatomic particles to do certain tasks and calculations

## QWERTY

**KWUR *tee* • *noun***

a type of keyboard layout that features the letters Q, W, E, R, T, and Y as the first six letters of the second row (see What Kind of a Word Is QWERTY?, opposite)

## RAM

**RAAM • *noun***

stands for: **random-access memory**

a computer system's short-term memory, used to store calculation data

## RANDOM

**RAN *dum* • *adjective***

describes a function in a program that allows unpredictable outcomes

## REGISTER

**REH *jih stir* • *noun***

a place in a processor where data can be stored while it is being used for quick access by the computer

## RELATIONAL DATABASE

*reh LAY shun al – DAY tuh bayse • noun*

a place to store information in tables, made up of rows and fields; the most common type of database

---

### What Kind of a Word Is QWERTY?

Here's a hint: It has nothing to do with the alphabet. So how did we end up with QWERTY as the primary keyboard layout?

Christopher Latham Sholes did not initially include QWERTY in his typewriter design in the 1860s and 1870s. A myth says that this layout was developed to slow typists down because the early typewriters couldn't process inputs very quickly and the machines would get hung up. However, telegraph operators were among the first users of the typewriter, and they needed to transcribe messages quickly. They are responsible for the evolution of key placement to the current QWERTY design.

Other keyboard designs exist but have not been as ubiquitous or universally used. One such keyboard is the Dvorak Simplified Keyboard, which groups vowels on the left. Why is QWERTY the most popular design now? Maybe because everyone learns how to type this way!

## RELIABLE SOURCE

*rih LY uh bul – SORSE • noun*

a place where you can get information that can be trusted to be correct and/or objective and unbiased

*\*It's important to know if the source you are using can be trusted! Unreliable sources can help misinformation spread and can even be unsafe. (See Seven Questions to Help You Identify a Reliable Source, page 40.)*

## RESOLUTION

*reh sah LOO shun • noun*

the number of pixels (see page 34) that a display monitor contains, or a measure of how much information a file can hold

## RIGHT-CLICK

*RYTE-klihk • noun*

to press and release the right (or secondary) button on a mouse; a right-click action usually shows you a menu or the properties of whatever you clicked on

## ROBOT

*ROH baht • noun*

a computer that can perform tasks all by itself

*\*A robot can resemble a human, but many do not, such as a robot that helps people put cars together at a manufacturing plant or a robot that vacuums your house.*

## ROBOTICS

*roh BAH tiks • noun*

the study of robots

# ROM

**ROHM** • *noun*

stands for: **Read-Only Memory**

long-term storage for data that the computer needs for basic functions; *read-only* means that the memory cannot be changed, such as for a cartridge-based video game or a car

# ROUTER

**RAU** *tur* • *noun*

a device that sends data across a network; a wireless router is a device that can send an internet connection from a modem (see page 29) across a local area network

# RSS FEED

**are ess ESS – FEED** • *noun*

stands for: **Rich Site Summary** or **Really Simple Syndication**

a post or information that a website sends to a list of subscribers in an app or a web reader

# RUN

**RUHN** • *verb*

to make a program start; also called *execute*

## Seven Questions to Help You Identify a Reliable Source

1. Who is the author of this information?

2. How would they know and how would they have gotten this information?

3. Where was this information shared?

4. What is the purpose of sharing it?

5. Is there an an agenda, or a reason they might want to share this information?

6. When was this information last updated?

7. Can you find another source that reports on this information?

Other tips: While researching, look up the author or look up the organization where you found the information. And keep on your investigative hat—notice anything that seems fishy or potentially false.

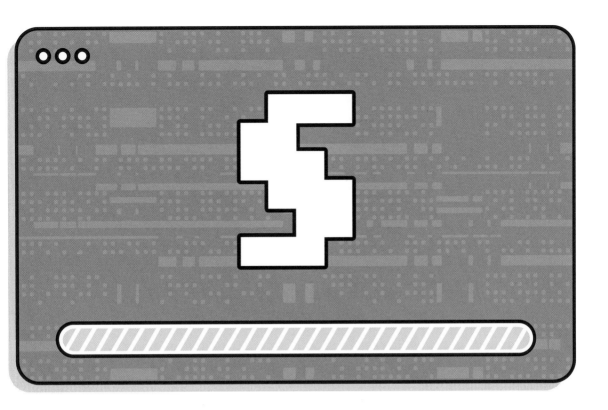

## SCANNER
**SKAA nuhr • noun**

an external hardware input device that copies an image, drawing, or body of text to a digital file so that it can be viewed on a computer

## SCREENSAVER
**SKREEN say ver • noun**

an image or graphic that replaces the desktop display after a computer has not been used for a set period of time

## SEARCH ENGINE
**SERCH – EN juhn • noun**

a program or software that is used to find information on a database or the world wide web

## SEMICONDUCTOR
**seh mee kon DUK ter • noun**

the brains of a computer; made from pure elements like silicon or germanium, material that can conduct electricity, which allows it to serve as the base for electronics

*Semiconductors hold billions of transistors, tiny switches that control electron flow through a circuit.*

## SEO
**ess ee OH • noun**

stands for: **Search Engine Optimization**

the process of using words and phrases that will drive more people to visit your website

Even things that seem invisible, like the internet, can have a big effect on the environment. Many websites and services depend on a large number of servers (see below). They all live on a server farm, a massive data center with lots of computers that are always on. These buildings get really hot because of the computer activity and need to be cooled down to stay working. They use a lot of power and energy.

Where are these data centers? Usually in an area where there's lots of space. Facebook's server farm is in Oregon. Northern Virginia is home to some of Amazon's.

## SEQUENCE

**SEE kwense • noun**

the primary structure and order of programs or algorithms

## SERVER

**SIR vur • noun**

a computer that provides information and services (like storage) to other computers over a network (like the internet); when a user visits a website, the information is sent from the website's server to the user across the network (see Not THAT Kind of Farm, above)

## SHORTCUT

**SHORT kut • noun**

a link or a record that provides a quick way to access a program or file

## SILICON

**SIH lih kon or SIH lih kin • noun**

a chemical element (Si) that occurs naturally in the earth's crust and can be used to make semiconductors (see From Crust to Wafer, opposite)

## SMS

**ess em ESS • noun**

stands for: **Short Message Service**

commonly known as texting, SMS sends messages over phone lines instead of the internet; it can connect any phone to almost any other phone but has privacy issues since it cannot be encrypted

*If you send a media file like a photo or video via text, that's called MMS: Multimedia Messaging Service*

## SOCIAL MEDIA

**SOH shul – ME dee ya • noun**

a network where people can create profiles and connect with other users to share text, images, and videos (see The Pros and Cons of Social Media, pages 36–37)

## SOCIAL MEDIA BUBBLE

**SOH shul – ME dee ya – BUH bul • noun phrase**

an algorithmic bias (see page 1) that causes all the information that you get from social media and the posts you see to be representative of a similar perspective

*This can also be called an echo chamber or filter bubble. Your filter can change or become more well-rounded if you intentionally seek out different or new points of view.*

## SOCKET

**SOK it • noun**

a two-way connection point

## SOFTWARE

**SAWFT ware • noun**

The instructions or programs that tell a computer, application, tool, or something similar what to do or how to perform a task; a broad term that means anything that isn't hardware

## SOUND CARD

**SOWND – KARD • noun**

a device for producing sound on a computer that is usually built into the motherboard

## SPAM

**SPAM • noun**

a word that describes junk email, bulk email, postings, or communication that is unasked for, often coming from an account or source you don't know

*Spam can be seen as a potential scam. It could be as harmless as an ad from a company you didn't want to hear from or as harmful as someone looking for money or a program attempting to infect your computer with a virus.*

## SPEAKER

**SPEE kur • noun**

a hardware device that lets a computer produce sounds

## SPRITE

**SPRYT • noun**

a two-dimensional image that can be moved, like a flat video game character

## SPYWARE

**SPEYE ware • noun**

software that is used to secretly gather information about a person or their activities

---

### From Crust to Wafer

A semiconductor is the building block of every computer. And semiconductors are made from elements like silicon. This element is present in the earth's crust in large quantities—it's the second most abundant element after oxygen!

A rock called quartz is made up of silicon components, but silicon is also present in sand. Silicon-rich sand can be melted and cooled to form a solid, which then gets sliced into wafers (see page 51).

Even though silicon is an abundant resource, mining the element has a major carbon footprint, and gases emitted by the creation of chips also have a negative impact on the climate.

## SQL

**ess cue EL • noun**

stands for: **Structured Query Language**

a standardized language that is used to work with databases

## SSD

**ess ess DEE • noun**

stands for: **Solid State Drive**

a storage device that connects to a computer and can store data even when it's not connected to the computer, like a flash drive

## STATEMENT

**STAYTE mint • noun**

the smallest instruction that you can give a programming language

## STREAM

**STREEM • verb**

to watch video on the internet

## STRING

**STRING • noun**

a group of characters; strings can contain numbers, letters, words, or symbols, such as a colon

## STYLUS

**STYE luhs • noun**

a pen especially made for use on a trackpad to move the cursor (see page 11)

## SURVEILLANCE

**surh VAY lentz • noun**

when someone or something is closely observing or watching you or your activity online

## SWITCH

**SWIHTCH • noun**

the mechanical button under a keycap of a keyboard that registers when you press the keycap

## SYNTAX

**SIN taks • noun**

the rules that define how a program must be structured so that a computer can read the code

## SYNTHETIC MEDIA

**sin THEH tik – ME dee ya • noun**

media that's produced by technology, like a movie script written by artificial intelligence

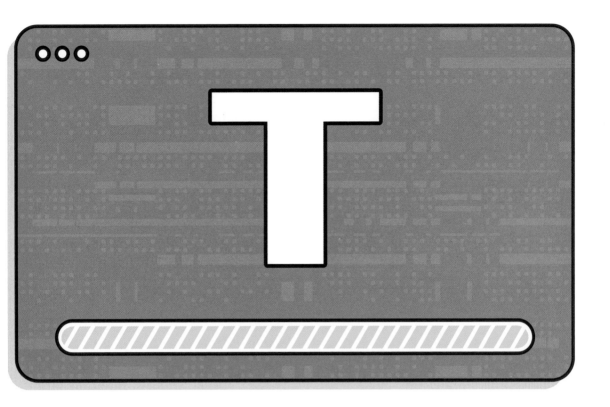

## TABLET

**TAHB let • noun**

a small portable computer that features a touchscreen as the primary way users can interact with it

## TAG

**TAG • noun**

a keyword or phrase that is assigned to a piece of information and helps provide details about it

## TASKBAR

**TASK bahr • noun**

a bar on the bottom or side of a desktop display that helps the user easily access applications or documents

## TCP/IP

**tee cee pee / EYE pee • noun**

stands for: **Transmission Control Protocol/ Internet Protocol**

the internet protocol suite, a set of rules that are used in networks such as the internet to make sure data ends up in the right place within the network

## TERMINAL

**TUR mih nul • noun**

an interface that allows the user to type commands and run programs by communicating directly with the computer through text

## TOUCHSCREEN

**TUCH skreen • noun**

a display screen that is also a touch-sensitive surface, allowing the user to interact directly with the items on the screen

A B C D E F G H I J K L M N O P Q R S (T) U V W X Y Z

## TRACKPAD

**TRAK pahd • noun**

a touch-sensitive surface that allows the user to use their fingers or a stylus (see page 44) to move the cursor; it can be built into a laptop or a separate hardware device

## TRAFFIC

**TRA fick • noun**

the overall users on a network at a particular time, such as the number of visitors going to a website or web page

## TRANSISTOR

**tran ZIS ter • noun**

a device that is used to maintain the flow of electric current

## TRANSLATOR

**TRANS lay tor • noun**

any program or processor that converts one computer language into a different computer language; for example, translating programming language into machine code (see From Letters to Numbers, opposite)

## TROJAN

**TROH shjun • noun**

malware or malicious code that pretends to be another piece of software to trick the user and damage or steal from their computer; also called a *Trojan horse*

*This malware gets its name from a Greek myth. In the story, the Greeks wanted to get into the city of Troy, but it was heavily barricaded. So they created a giant wooden horse that was hollow and a handful of Greek soldiers hid inside. When the Trojans brought it into their city, thinking it was a gift, the Greeks emerged and let their army into the gates.*

## T Is for Typing

Typing, or using your fingers to hit keys on a keyboard, seems very straightforward, but it can be done in more than one way. Here are a few words related to typing:

- **Hunt and peck:** a method of typing where you look for the keys with your eyes before pressing them with your fingers
- **Touch typing:** using all of your fingers on the keyboard without having to look at the keys
- **Thumbing:** using both thumbs to press the keys on a smaller, handheld device
- **WPM:** words per minute, or how many words you can type in a minute

## TROLL

**TROHL • noun**

someone who is mean or rude with the intention to harm or offend others online

## TROUBLESHOOT

**TRUH buhl shoot • verb**

to figure out solutions to a problem, sometimes via a process like trial and error

## TURING TEST

**TUR ing – TEST • noun**

a test given to a computer to determine its intelligence and especially its ability to mimic human intelligence

*This test was created by Alan Turing, who called it the Imitation Game (read his bio on page 16).*

---

## From Letters to Numbers

Computers talk to each other through numbers. So how do we get human languages to be translated into computer-speak? Through a translator—something that converts one computer language into another (for example, a programming language into machine code). There are several different types of translation:

**↓ HUMAN ↓**
WORDS AND LANGUAGE LIKE ENGLISH OR JAPANESE

**↓ HIGH-LEVEL ↑**
PROGRAMMING LANGUAGES LIKE JAVA, C, C++

*High-level languages are closer to human languages. These languages get converted and compiled into an assembly language (see below) by a compiler or an interpreter.*

A compiler and an interpreter build the technical machine code for you as part of their programming. So a programming language can be applied to any type of machine, and the compiler or interpreter can translate it to the machine level.

**↓ LOW-LEVEL ↑**
ASSEMBLY LANGUAGE

*An assembler converts assembly language into machine code or binary. Because the assembler is making machine code, the code or instructions will be different for each operating system.*

**↓ MACHINE CODE ↑**

*A low-level language is like the alphabet. The letters don't mean much on their own, but when combined, they form words (a higher-level language).*

**↑ THE COMPUTER HARDWARE ↑**
BINARY

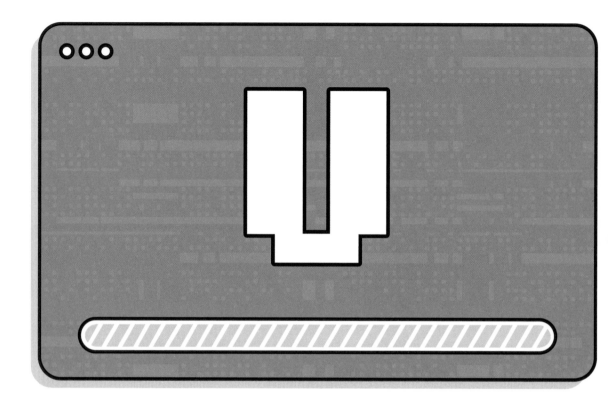

## UI

**yew EYE • noun**

stands for: **user interface**

the part of an application that a person (or user) interacts with

## UNCANNY VALLEY

**uhn CAN ee – VAH lee • noun**

the idea that there is a point at which artificial intelligence is so close to human form that it starts to look weird or eerie to humans

## UNICODE

**YEW nih cohd • noun**

the standard everywhere for translating all symbols and characters in every language so that computers can read and use them

## UPDATE

**UHP dayte • noun**

new code that is pushed out, or released, to fix bugs or add features to an application or software that you already have on your device

*Always make sure your devices are set to automatically update. Bug fixes can correct serious security risks, and you want to make sure you're staying safe!*

## UPGRADE

**UHP grayd • noun**

a new version of software that will replace an older version

A B C D E F G H I J K L M N O P Q R S T U V W X Y Z

## UPLOAD
**UHP load • *noun or verb***

refers to data being sent from a computer to the internet or a device

## URL
**yew are ELL • *noun***

stands for: **Uniform Resource Locator**

the address where a webpage or file can be found on the internet; also called a *web address*

## USB
**yew ess BEE • *noun***

stands for: **Universal Serial Bus**

a port with a cable that can connect devices so that they can communicate with each other

## USER
**YEW zer • *noun***

a person who interacts with a computer

## USERNAME
**YEW zer naym • *noun***

a name that you use to identify yourself to log in to a website or program

## UX
**yew EX • *noun***

stands for: **user experience**

the overall impression someone has while using an application or system, especially how easy or frustrating it is to use; also called *UE*

*The UX is the type of experience someone has while working with the UI.*

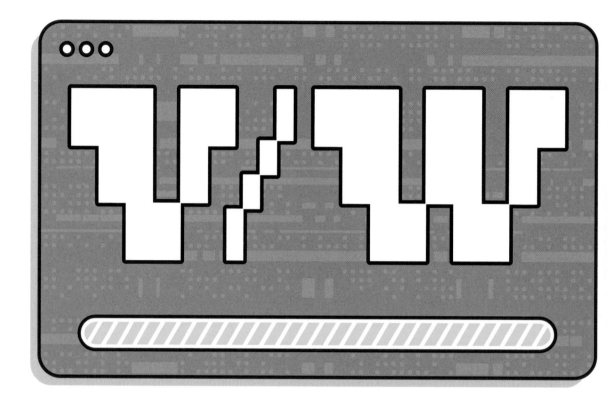

## VALUE

**VAL yew • noun**

the representation of something; the information that can be stored in a container

## VARIABLE

**VA ree ah bul • noun**

a value that can change; a container that can hold information or values

## VIDEO CARD

**VIH dee oh – KAHRD • noun**

hardware that lets a computer send video signals to an external output device that can display images, like a monitor; also called a graphics card, a display or video adapter, or a video controller

## VIRTUAL REALITY

**VIHR choo wuhl – ree AA lih tee • noun**

an artificial three-dimensional image or environment that a user can interact with, created using a computer

## VIRUS

**VEYE russ • noun**

a type of malicious program, or malware (see page 28), that is designed to replicate itself and spread from one device to another; for example, a virus can steal your data or damage or corrupt a device so that it's harder or impossible to use (see Going Viral, opposite)

## VISUALIZATION

**VIH zhoo wal ih zay shun • noun**

the use of graphics to display information

# VISUAL LANGUAGE

VIH zhoo wal – LAN gwij • noun

any programming language that lets the user create instructions using graphics instead of text; Scratch is a good example

# WAFER

WAY fur • noun

a thin piece of semiconductor material, like silicon crystal, shaped like a disc; used to manufacture chips and other tiny electronic devices

*Some wafers can be as big as a large pizza!

# WALLPAPER

WAHL pay pur • noun

also known as the background on a computer's desktop; a user can change it to display whatever image they prefer

# WEARABLE

WARE uh bul • noun

an electronic device that can be worn on the body and functions like an accessory, such as a watch or medical alert monitor. Some wearables can be implanted in the body or tattooed on the skin!

# WEB PAGE

WEHB – payj • noun

a single document displayed on the world wide web through a browser

# WEBSITE

WEHB syt • noun

a destination on the world wide web that is made up of multiple web pages (see above) and connected via a home page; also called *site* for short

# WETWARE

WEHT ware • noun

a computer made up of organic material, like cells

# WI-FI

WIY–fie • noun

wireless network technology that can connect multiple electronic devices to the internet through radio waves

*Wi-Fi seems like it's an abbreviation, but it doesn't stand for anything! A marketing firm made up the name when the creators of the technology, which was originally called IEEE 802.11, needed something catchier for their product.

## WINDOW

**WIHN doh • noun**

an area on the computer desktop that contains and displays information

## WINDOW MANAGER

**WIHN doh – MAN ah jer • noun**

software that determines what the windows on a desktop look like and how they can be used

## WORD PROCESSOR

**WURD – PRAH seh sohr • noun**

a computer software program that allows the user to create and compose documents

---

### The Internet or the Web?

Even though we talk mostly about looking things up "on the internet," the pages that you see online are actually the world wide web. But the internet is HOW you see them; it's the network that connects all of the many computers that are online and allows you to see the information on the pages.

It's as if the internet is a giant bookstore and the world wide web is all of the books within the store.

---

## WORLD WIDE WEB

**WIRLD – WIID – WEHB • noun**

an information system or application of web pages that can be found using an address; or, all of the web pages that can be seen using the internet

*Those three letters at the beginning of a website—www—stand for world wide web. The web was developed by Sir Tim Berners-Lee at a European physics lab in 1989.*

---

### Y2K: The End of the World? (Clearly Not!)

In the year 1999, the citizens of earth were in a panic about the Y2K bug. Also known as the millennium bug, it was a glitch in computer programs predicted to cause massive disruptions throughout systems everywhere. The problem was that the first computer programmers omitted the first two digits in the four-digit year, so many people thought that in all computer systems everywhere, the 00 in the year 2000 would be interpreted as 1900 and the time variation would cause havoc. When the clock struck midnight on January 1, 2000, the result was pretty anti-climactic—there were very few issues, even in countries that had not spent lots of money updating to the four-digit year.

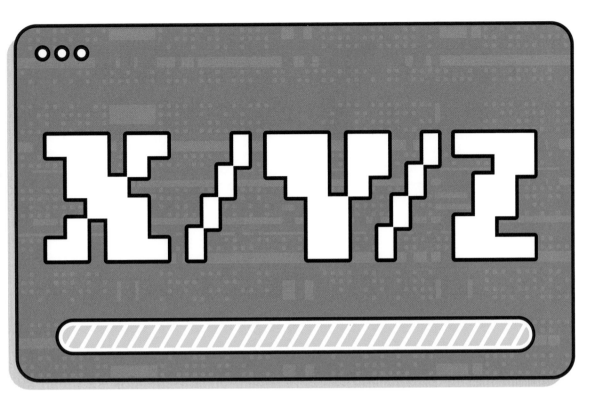

## XML

**ex em EL • noun**

short for: **Extensible Markup Language**

a language for representing data that can be understood by a computer

*\*Related to HTML (see page 23), XML is used to store data and move it around, rather than tell the computer how to display the data, which is what HTML does.*

## YOKE

**YOHK • noun**

a hardware input device that looks like the control column for steering a plane. It has a handle that moves up/down and back/forth to run flight simulations.

## ZERO

**ZEE roh • noun**

a number used to represent "false" to a computer

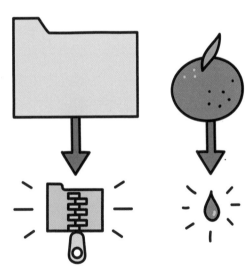

## ZIP FILE

**ZIHP – FYL • noun**

a file that ends in .ZIP is a compressed file, or a file with a reduced size; zipped files take up less space in storage, and smaller files can also be transferred more easily from one location to another

# Tech Timeline

## Some Important Events in Computer Science History

**1834:**

Charles Babbage starts work on the Analytical Engine.

**1843:**

Ada Lovelace unknowingly publishes the first algorithm (see page 1).

**1939:**

Hewlett-Packard, the producer of the world's first personal computer, is founded.

**1943:**

British code breakers successfully test the Colossus Mark 1, a programmable digital cipher.

**1954:**

IBM presents a revolutionary electronic calculator made with transistors and integrated circuits.

**1958:**

"Tennis for Two," one of the first electronic multiplayer video games, is born.

**1971:**

Ray Tomlinson sends the first email.

**1973:**

The first portable cell phone call is made.

**1894:**

Thomas Edison makes the first cat video, "The Boxing Cats."

**1937:**

A device called the "Model K" Adder provides proof that Boolean logic can be applied to computers.

**1946:**

The ENIAC computer (see page 17) is presented to the public.

**1950:**

Alan Turing (see page 16) comes up with the Turing Test, a measure of a machine's intelligence.

**1962:**

J.C.R. Licklider comes up with the idea for an "Intergalactic Computer Network" that links computers located in different places—the precursor to the internet.

**1973:**

Robert Kahn and Vinton Cerf develop a protocol (TCP/IP, see page 45) for linking multiple networks together.

**1983:**

The term "Internet" is coined.

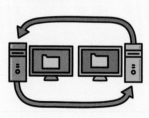

## 1985:

The first domain is registered.

## 1989:

Sir Tim Berners-Lee imagines the first version of the world wide web.

## 1997:

Wi-Fi is released to consumers.

## 2004:

TheFacebook.com launches at Harvard University.

## 2009:

Google's self-driving car project launches.

## 2010:

Siri, the first virtual assistant, is unveiled by Apple.

## 2011:

IBM's computer named Watson defeats two of the best champions of *Jeopardy!*

## 2015:

Google DeepMind's AlphaGo program beats Go champion Fan Hui.

## 2016:

Millions of people take to the streets to play the augmented reality game Pokémon Go.

## 1995:

Microsoft launches Windows 95; Amazon, Yahoo, eBay, and mp3s are all born.

## 1996:

Google is founded in a garage near Stanford University.

## 2005:

Founder Jawed Karim uploads "Me at the Zoo," the first YouTube video.

## 2007:

The iPhone is born.

## 2008:

The cryptocurrency Bitcoin is invented.

## 2012:

A Kickstarter campaign for the virtual reality headset Oculus raises $2.4 million.

## 2014:

Denmark creates a virtual version of the entire country within the game of Minecraft.

## 2020:

Videoconferencing platforms like Zoom skyrocket in popularity due to a global pandemic.

## 2021:

Twitter founder Jack Dorsey's first tweet (from 2006) is sold as an NFT.

# FURTHER BROWSING

*There are many resources on the internet where you can learn more about the subjects covered in this book! Here are a few of our favorites:*

*Code.org*

*Khan Academy*

*Girls Who Code*

*Black Girls Code*

*Elon University, Imagining the Internet elon.edu/u/imagining/*

*Scratch*

*TypingClub or Jungle Junior (websites to practice typing)*

*Stop Bullying.gov*

*Robotics Alliance Project at Nasa.gov*

*\*These website addresses were accurate at the time this book went to press. Always make sure to check information online for accuracy and reliability.*

# GREAT OFFLINE READS

*Ada Byron Lovelace and the Thinking Machine*
by Laurie Wallmark

*Big Data: Information in the Digital World with Science Activities*
by Carla Mooney and Alexis Cornell

*But I Read It on the Internet!* by Toni Buzzeo

*Can You Crack the Code? A Fascinating History of Ciphers
and Cryptography* by Ella Schwartz

*Coding Games in Scratch* by Jon Woodcock

*Everything You Need to Ace Computer
Science and Coding in One Big
Fat Notebook* by Grant Smith

*The Extraordinary Life of Katherine Johnson* by Devika Jina

*Get Coding! Learn HTML, CSS, and JavaScript and Build a Website,
App, and Game* by Young Rewired State

*Girls Who Code: Learn to Code and Change
the World* by Reshma Saujani

*hello! hello!* by Matthew Cordell

*The History of the Computer: People,
Inventions, and Technology that Changed
Our World* by Rachel Ignotofsky

*Machine Learning for Kids* by Dale Lane

*The Technology Tail: A Digital Footprint Story* by Julia Cook

*Troll Stinks* by Jeanne Willis

Library of Congress Cataloging-in-Publication Data available upon request.

ISBN: 978-1-955834-15-5

duopress books are available at special discounts when purchased in
bulk for sales promotions as well as for fundraising or educational use.
Special editions can be created to specification.
Contact us at hello@duopressbooks.com for more information.

Manufactured in China
10 9 8 7 6 5 4 3 2 1
Duo Press LLC. 8 Market Place, Suite 300, Baltimore, MD 21202

Design and art direction by Alyssa Nassner
Editing by Liz Saunders
Copyediting by Michele Suchomel-Casey

To order: hello@duopressbooks.com
www.duopressbooks.com